Thesiger's Ret

by Peter Clark

Black and white photography
by Wilfred Thesiger

*Published with
the support and
encouragement of
BP Exploration*

MOTIVATE
PUBLISHING

Published by
Motivate Publishing

PO Box 2331
Dubai, UAE
Tel: 824060
Fax: 824436

PO Box 43072
Abu Dhabi, UAE
Tel: 311666
Fax: 311888

London House
26/40, Kensington High Street
London W8 4PF
Tel: 071 937 4024
Fax: 071 937 7293

Directors:
Obaid Humaid Al Tayer
Ian Fairservice

Senior Editor:
Julia Roles

Art Director:
Mark Pettipher

ISBN 1 873544 36 7

Printed by Emirates Printing Press, Dubai

Contents

To
Musallim bin Al Kamam
the Third Musketeer

Cover: A study of Wilfred Thesiger. (Alan Hillyer)
Title page: The hawking party. (39/7/14 R)
This page: Bin Kabina bringing camel fodder — 1948. (99/9/17)

Preface

On a cool February night in 1990, a small group gathered at Abu Dhabi international airport to await the regular Gulf Air flight from Nairobi. The airport was quiet, its army of workers idling before the nightly onslaught of travellers from all points of the compass whose flight paths intersected here: A few frantic midnight hours when dozens of planes and thousands of passengers would transit this modern-day Arabian oasis; jumbo jets where once there were camels, sun-burnt tourists where once there were weather-beaten Bedu.

The Nairobi flight touched down without fanfare. It might have come and gone almost unnoticed, a tramp steamer in an ocean liner's world, except for the fact that this night it was carrying Wilfred Thesiger back to Arabia. This was the man, hailed as one of the greatest living explorers for his travels in Arabia, Africa and the Subcontinent, who more than 40 years previously had arrived in the middle of these same dunes and islands the hard way, overland, from the awe-inspiring Empty Quarter; and in so doing, had become a legend.

Here he was in person, tall, gaunt and surprisingly athletic for his 80 years, back where it all began, the official guest of the Abu Dhabi government. The airport's VIP lounge was at his disposal. "Frankly," he mused privately, "I'm surprised they let me in." Indeed, years earlier some might have protested his arrival, but the passage of time, like the blowing sands of the desert, smooths rough edges. Equally, many in Abu Dhabi might have been surprised that Thesiger, the outsider, the "stone age man" who wears his loathing of all things modern on his sleeve, actually chose to return…

Wilfred Thesiger's association with Arabia goes back to the late 1940s, half a lifetime for him and an eternity for the sheikhdoms, like Abu Dhabi, that he visited. His book *Arabian Sands*, which describes those years and is illustrated with his own remarkable black and white photos, remains a classic of informative travel writing. In it he presents an enduring and endearing image of traditional

Wilfred Thesiger in 1948 (left) and 1990; the man who was hailed as one of the greatest living explorers for his travels in Arabia.

Arab society with all its customs, courtesies and conventions, and above all the fellowship of his companions, forged through facing incredible hardship together. This was nobility in the raw.

Later expeditions into Iraq, Iran, Afghanistan, Pakistan and Ethiopia fed his appetite for challenge and adventure; numerous awards from learned associations such as the Royal Geographical Society, literary prizes and honorary degrees attest to the value attached to his wanderings. His was the good fortune to be able to pursue what he most enjoyed. In his autobiography *The Life of My Choice*, Thesiger writes: "Journeying at walking pace under conditions of some hardship, I was perhaps the last explorer in the tradition of the past. I was happiest when I had no

On the way to Oman.
Thesiger and his Arab companions roamed Oman and southern Arabia, travelling deep into the heart of the previously impregnable Empty Quarter.

communication with the outside world, when I was utterly dependent on my tribal companions."

But while Thesiger and his Arab companions roamed Oman and southern Arabia, travelling deep into the heart of the previously impregnable Empty Quarter with little more than their wits to live on, oilmen were nibbling at the peripheries, already on the scent of

the riches that would change the area and the lives of its people for ever. Although to Thesiger, the upper crust Englishman, the primitive life of the desert with all its deprivations and very real risks was infinitely preferable to that into which he was born, the indigenous Arab saw things differently.

Education and travel showed the Arabs that there was more to life than the constant battle of survival, and oil wealth gave them the means to achieve it remarkably fast. Where clusters of dusty coralstone huts once stood, gleaming office and apartment blocks now tower above lush green parks and gardens. All the trappings of modern civilisation were grafted onto the traditional society in a space of less than a generation.

In 1977, accepting a long-standing invitation from H.H. Sheikh Zayed bin Sultan Al Nahyan, Thesiger returned to Arabia after an absence of some 25 years. Searching for the past, he found something quite different. He did not like what he saw, and referred in print to Abu Dhabi as "an Arabian nightmare". Disillusioned, he went back to his remote corner of Kenya. There he remained, out of the public eye, until publication in 1987 of *The Life of My Choice* brought renewed interest from a generation that takes moon landings for granted. It took a special reason to entice him away from his chosen surroundings. Fortunately, in 1990, and again in 1991, just such reasons were found.

Thesiger has always maintained a home in London, and it was during one of his visits to England in 1989 that I had the privilege to dine with him one April evening at the Travellers' Club. I was then head of the British Council, the government-supported language and cultural centre, in the UAE and a long-time admirer of his work. At dinner he spoke of the solace he derived from going through the 70 albums of photographs accumulated on his travels. A fraction of these had been published in *Arabian Sands* and

"Journeying at walking pace under conditions of some hardship, I was perhaps the last explorer in the tradition of the past. I was happiest when I had no communication with the outside world, when I was utterly dependent on my tribal companions."

Visions of a Nomad, but I found myself thinking that there must be many more featuring scenes of the United Arab Emirates and Oman that had never been seen. Surely they would be of great interest, particularly to the people of the Emirates. Why not an exhibition of his photographs? Why not an exhibition held at the British Council? Why not indeed? The seed was sown.

During the following months, Thesiger gave me permission to arrange the exhibition, and in August my wife and I spent a morning at his Chelsea flat going through the albums and selecting pictures. I returned to Abu Dhabi, and Thesiger to Kenya from where he took an interest in arrangements for what was to be the first exhibition of his photographs — incredible, considering the historical importance and stark beauty of the work.

As all this was happening, in the back of my mind a thought persisted:

Street stall, Dubai — 1948.
Thesiger had 70 albums of photographs, including many of the United Arab Emirates and Oman that had never been seen.

"Would Thesiger himself ever consider...?" Yet I was reluctant to invite him. I was aware of his very negative feelings about the modern Arabia. His visit in 1977 had not been a happy experience and I had too much respect for the man to risk exposing him to further pain. But in December a friend of Thesiger's suggested he might consent, and his London agent seconded the opinion: "He hates hotels but provided he is well looked after, he may well love to come."

With only a little hesitation, I wrote to Thesiger at his hut in northern Kenya, faxing my letter to the British Council in Nairobi with the request that they somehow get it to him. I held my breath: This was the man who had written after his brief revisits to Oman and Abu Dhabi: "Present-day Arabia, with its prodigious wealth, had nothing whatever left to offer me." His reply came in early January — he would be happy to come. As his agent put it, Thesiger had "mellowed a lot".

"Present-day Arabia, with its prodigious wealth, had nothing whatever left to offer me."

9

A brave, awkward, attractive creature

There can be few people who have embodied from birth such extremes of human experience as has Wilfred Thesiger. Born into the English privileged class on an African outpost, he has commuted all his life between civilisation, as represented by London and rural England, and the Third World — Africa, Arabia and the Subcontinent. Remarkably, he has been able to maintain a personal equilibrium while journeying constantly between these two diametrically opposed worlds.

He was born on 3rd June, 1910, in a mud building on the compound of the British Mission in Addis Ababa, Abyssinia (now Ethiopia), where his father was head of the mission — effectively ambassador. For several generations the Thesigers had been prominent in British imperial service, in law and in soldiering. His great-grandfather was Lord Chancellor in a Disraeli cabinet; his grandfather was a general in the army; and his uncle, Lord Chelmsford, was viceroy of India and a minister in the first Labour cabinet. His mother, Mary, was Irish. Generous, warm, proud and sensitive, she was a focus for Thesiger's affections for most of his life. In his words, she "was fun to be with". The eldest of four brothers, he was named Wilfred after his father while his second name, Patrick, acknowledged the Irish strain on his mother's side.

Thesiger's first nine years were spent amid the barbaric splendour of Abyssinia. His father was an ally and personal friend of Ras Tafari, the future Emperor Haile Selassie, who was emerging victor after a ferocious civil war. Reverence for the person and memory of Haile Selassie was to remain a fixed point throughout Thesiger's life, while other childhood experiences made equally lasting impressions. In 1916, as a child of six, he observed a captive rebel army being paraded in humiliation in Addis Ababa. "I believe," he wrote in his autobiography *The Life of My Choice*, "that day implanted in me a life-long craving for barbaric splendour, for savagery and colour and the throb of drums, and that it gave me a lasting veneration for long-established custom and ritual, from which would derive later a deep-seated resentment of Western innovations in other lands, and a distaste for the drab uniformity of the modern world."

After such an extraordinary infancy, Thesiger spent the 1920s in England. His father died while he was at a

Left. Moving the family.
All his life, Thesiger has commuted between civilisation and the Third World.

Wilfred Thesiger in the saddle with his father in 1914 during a journey from Addis Ababa to the distant railhead.

DMM 15

preparatory school near Brighton and his mother struggled to provide a gentleman's education for each of her sons. Wilfred went to Eton which he loved. Years later he was to present the manuscript of *Arabian Sands* to the Eton College Library. He went on to Magdalen College, Oxford, where he read modern history for a degree, and books about big game hunting for fun, and boxed as a light heavyweight for the university. His British base was a roomy house his mother rented near Knighton, on the borders of Shropshire, within walking distance of some of the least developed parts of southern Britain.

The young Thesiger had difficulty adjusting to his English contemporaries. He was ignorant about the finer points of cricket and must have appeared a sensitive, distracted loner. He read and dreamed about Africa, adventure and the lives of the great explorers, devouring the novels of Joseph Conrad, John Buchan and Rudyard Kipling.

While still an undergraduate, he returned to Abyssinia. Haile Selassie, remembering the support and sympathy he had received from Thesiger's parents, invited him to attend his coronation, and Thesiger travelled out in the entourage of the son of King George V, the Duke of Gloucester. After the coronation he made his first wanderings in remoter Abyssinia. Three years later he made his first major journey of exploration, in the Danakil country in eastern Abyssinia where he was the first European to travel through the Aussa

Danakil country 1933-34 — A crossing.

During his first major journey of exploration, in the Danakil country in eastern Abyssinia, he was the first European to travel through the Aussa Sultanate and live to tell the tale.

Sultanate and live to tell the tale. As with later expeditions, mapping and collecting zoological specimens gave his journeys a scientific, albeit for Thesiger, secondary purpose. The real reason, as he recounted in his autobiography, had more to do with staring his own mortality in the face.

In the Aussa Sultanate he and his African retainers found themselves alone with the sultan who had a reputation for ruthless and wilful cruelty. "As I looked round the clearing at the ranks of squatting warriors and the small isolated group of my own men, I knew that this moonlight meeting in unknown Africa with a savage potentate who hated Europeans was the realisation of my boyhood dreams. I had come here in search of adventure: the mapping, the

collecting of animals and birds were all incidental. The knowledge that somewhere in this neighbourhood three previous expeditions had been exterminated, that we were far beyond any hope of assistance, that even our whereabouts were unknown, I found wholly satisfying."

In 1935 he joined the Sudan Political Service, that body of men which administered the Anglo-Egyptian Sudan. He was posted to Kutum in Darfur in the remote far west of the country as assistant district commissioner, working with a remarkable man called Guy Moore. Moore had served in Iraq after the First World War and was a stimulating conversationalist with views that fitted ill with those of the earnest improvers of the country, but which coincided with those of Thesiger. Neither had any sense of imperial mission to uplift and modernise the lives of the people they were sent to administer. They both recognised that the Sudanese were perfectly capable of conducting their own affairs without the meddling interference of the likes of Moore and Thesiger. "We were well aware," Thesiger recalled 50 years later, "of the disruption which must ensue from the wholesale intrusion of an alien education into their society, with the consequent breakdown of family life, drift to the towns, unemployment and discontent. That this was ultimately inevitable we recognised; we merely wished, in all good faith, to defer these consequences as long as possible."

From Kutum he travelled to the deserts to the north and became familiar with camels, desert life and his travelling companions with whom he spoke only in Arabic. Unlike most other imperial officials who kept themselves racially and personally aloof, Thesiger learnt to live the lives of his Sudanese companions, to travel light, sleep rough and eat off the land. Practising this form of social psychology before it had a name was to become a hallmark of Thesiger's travels and a major factor in his

"As I looked round the clearing at the ranks of squatting warriors and the small isolated group of my own men, I knew that this moonlight meeting in unknown Africa with a savage potentate who hated Europeans was the realisation of my boyhood dreams."

Khartoum — December 1940.
Thesiger talking to Haile Selassie at the beginning of the campaign to liberate Abyssinia.

successful integration into other cultures. It stemmed not from a rejection of his own roots, but rather directly from pride in his own race and the traditions of his family and country uncorrupted into any sense of racial superiority. Just as he cherished his own Britishness, so he appreciated and respected the integrity and pride of others in their heritage and culture.

After a couple of years in Darfur, Thesiger was transferred to the area of the Western Nuer in the Upper Nile province. The Nuer had avoided Arabisation and Islamisation and retained their own very distinctive letterless culture based on cows. Thesiger spent much time on steamers travelling from river settlement to river settlement, hunting lions and enjoying the sense of remoteness. As an administrator he was not likely to shine in Khartoum. He was not besotted by paperwork and most of the official mail that arrived was thrown overboard. It was people that mattered. He respected many of his colleagues and especially the head of the Sudan Political Service, Sir Douglas Newbold, who drove himself to an early death working competently and modestly for the welfare of the Sudanese.

Newbold recorded that Thesiger realised he was a misfit, but "a misfit only in a government and owing to an excess of certain ancient virtues, and not because of any vices — a brave, awkward, attractive creature."

During Thesiger's Sudan years, Abyssinia was invaded by Italy and Haile Selassie was exiled to Britain, where he lived in Bath. Thesiger felt a bitter hatred towards the Italians. When the Second World War broke out he could not wait to be involved in a campaign to restore Haile Selassie. Typically, his career during the war was remarkable. He was involved in three theatres — Abyssinia, Syria and North Africa. In all three his service was unconventional, individualistic, heroic and an apt prelude to his years in southern Arabia.

In the autumn of 1939, Thesiger was given a commission in the Sudan Defence Force, but he had to wait until June 1940 before he heard any shots fired in anger. He was posted to the Sudan/Abyssinia border and on 10th June heard on the radio that Britain and Italy were at war. "We greeted the broadcast by firing our machine gun into the Italian positions." Later he received an order

Druze elders.
Thesiger spent several weeks visiting villages of the Druze, contributing to the defeat of the Vichy French in July 1941.

that under no (repeat no) circumstances were any units to take any offensive action without permission from headquarters. But it gave Thesiger immense satisfaction to have fired the first British shots against the Italians.

Thesiger entered Abyssinia, accompanied by one guide and three camels, made contact with local leaders and harried the Italians. During his 11 months in Abyssinia he was loosely attached to Orde Wingate, a most unconventional soldier, simultaneously brilliant and repulsive. Wingate, with singleminded drive, overran Italian garrisons and escorted Haile Selassie to his restoration at Addis Ababa.

After the success of the Abyssinian campaign, Thesiger was ordered to Cairo. He volunteered for service in Syria. In 1941, Syria was held by Vichy France. A British advance from the south was held up at Deraa and the British military authorities thought it would be a good idea if the Vichy French withdrawal were to be hastened by a revolt of the Druze, people of the mountains of southern Syria. Thesiger had spent holidays in the Thirties travelling in rural Syria and was ordered to assist in raising a Druze Legion. Based at the Syrian town of Malha, in Jabal Druze, Thesiger spent several weeks visiting villages of the Druze and contributing

to the final defeat of the Vichy French in July 1941. During this campaign Thesiger met the Bedu of Arabia for the first time.

Although the Free French resumed control of Syria, there were fears of a German invasion. Thesiger's military position was somewhat irregular. He belonged to no regular army unit, although he held the rank of Major. But he took orders from Special Operations Executive (SOE) who ordered him to prepare to stay behind in Syria in the event of a German occupation and to organise resistance through sabotage and the rallying of anti-German elements.

For several months, Thesiger's task was to wander around the country, examine points of potential vulnerability, such as railway bridges or mountain passes, identify prospective allies and in general be as familiar with Syria and its people as possible. He was joined in this task by a 24-year-old Lieutenant, Edward Henderson, who was to remain a lifelong friend — in 1990, nearly half a century later, Henderson was on hand to welcome Thesiger back to the UAE. But the agreeable task of travelling freely about Syria came to an end as German armies were bogged down in Russia and the threat of invasion receded. So Thesiger was recalled to Cairo in May 1942.

Thesiger then wanted to join the

Edward Henderson, right, a lifelong friend since they campaigned together in Syria during World War II, was on hand to welcome Thesiger back to the UAE in 1990. Here they are seen with H.E. Mr Ahmad Khalifa Al Suwaidi.

83/19/12

Long Range Desert Patrol to operate behind the enemy lines in north Africa, and by luck, he was recruited by David Stirling, the young Colonel who founded the Special Air Services (SAS), to join that highly mobile force operating in the area of north Africa occupied by the Germans. In November, Thesiger was off again on active service.

The SAS had several patrols, each with two jeeps. The patrols travelled well to the south and then to the east, avoiding the armies that hugged the coast. Success in these operations depended on coping with desert life and cooperating with the people of the desert. The SAS travelled through unmapped desert lands and carried out their actions at night. It was a life that required a minimum of discipline and maximum of personal initiative, physical hardship and actual danger.

Thesiger was in charge of a unit comprising himself, one other officer and two signallers with wireless equipment, and for six months they shot up German convoys, even invading enemy camps. The SAS activities distracted the enemy by dealing sudden and demoralising blows, forcing the Germans to dilute

their strength to deal with them. In so doing, the SAS provided essential support to Montgomery's advance along the north African coast with the Eighth Army.

After the fall of Tunis to the Allies in May 1943, Thesiger returned to Cairo and was released from military service: Emperor Haile Selassie had specifically asked for him to act as adviser to his son, Crown Prince Asfa Wossen, ruler of the Wollo area to the north of Addis Ababa. Thesiger was in Wollo throughout 1944; for him it was the most frustrating year of his life. He was away from the fields of military action, in a routine job which inhibited him from regular contact with the Abyssinian people. In early 1945 he resigned, depressed.

Then at a dinner in Addis Ababa, he met O B Lean of the Desert Locust Research Organisation, who wanted a man to look for locust outbreak centres in the deserts of southern Arabia. Thesiger seized the opportunity.

The war years had prepared him well for his travels in Arabia. Thesiger was physically fit, capable of pushing his body to the limits of duress. He had learned how to survive in deserts

Crossing the sands — 1948.
Thesiger had learned how to survive in deserts and had an instinctive rapport with desert people.

and had an instinctive rapport with desert people, remote from towns and those trappings of Western civilisation that he loathed — cars, planes, radio, telephones and cinemas. He appreciated the personal qualities that enabled a man to survive.

All his life Thesiger has been in search of adventure and worlds to explore. The pretext for entering Arabia was scientific research, but the opportunity was timely. The five years of travel in southern Arabia, summarised in the next chapter of this book, made his reputation. His account of those years, *Arabian Sands*, has become a classic of travel literature.

The 40 years after 1950 could have been an anticlimax, but Thesiger was presented with other adventures. In the autumn of 1950, he went for a fortnight's duck shooting in the marshes of Iraq, and ended up spending much of the next eight years there — with a break for exploring remotest Kurdistan — during which he became as acquainted with the lives of the Marsh Arabs as he had with the lives of the Bedu.

In the Fifties and Sixties, he travelled to remote parts of Iran, Afghanistan, Kurdistan and Pakistan. He returned to Abyssinia and, before the revolution in the Seventies which brought down Haile Selassie, explored most of the wilder parts of that country. He also wandered around northern Kenya and since 1968 has made his home at Maralal in the Samburu territory.

When he first arrived there, a 10-year-old Samburu boy named Lawi Leboyare attached himself to Thesiger. Lawi is now mayor of the town, and Thesiger, a respected father figure, has been 'adopted' by Lawi's family. He lives with them in great simplicity for nine months of the year, habitually

Left. The Marshes, near Zikri — 1958.
Thesiger became acquainted with the lives of the Marsh Arabs, as he had with the lives of the Bedu.

Baliki tents, Kurdistan — 1950.
In the Fifties and Sixties, he travelled to remote parts of Iran, Afghanistan, Kurdistan and Pakistan.

Gypsies with dancing bear — 1951.
The 40 years after 1950 could have been an anticlimax, but Thesiger was presented with other adventures.

Old Boys' match at Eton in 1933, with Wilfred Thesiger second from the right in the back row.

returning to London, to a flat in Chelsea, for the three summer months when he catches up with old friends and lunches almost daily at the Travellers' Club.

This pattern of life — nine months of the year in a hut in northern Kenya, wearing slacks and a bush shirt; and three months in London, wearing a three-piece suit and a

watch chain — reflects a curious dichotomy in Thesiger's life.

On the one hand he is a conservative, old-fashioned English gentleman. He feels strongly about the appropriateness of dress, and accepts tradition, hierarchy and the dictates of convention. As a young man, working his passage on a tramp steamer bound for the Black Sea, he

received an invitation to call on the British ambassador at Constantinople. Thesiger felt embarrassed at the prospect of meeting him. "I am conventional enough to dislike appearing anywhere in unsuitable clothes. Here I was wearing a shirt and an old pair of grey flannel trousers; they were clean, for I had washed them, but they were certainly not suitable for calling on an ambassador. However, I had nothing better on board and could not ignore his summons."

Moreover, he had a privileged upbringing. Few English children would even get to visit India, let alone stay with the viceroy with literally hundreds of servants to look after them. Eton College, which he

**Sunset in the Marshes —
1956.**
*Thesiger went for a fortnight's
duck shooting in the marshes
of Iraq, and ended up
spending much of the next
eight years there.*

1956/38/5

"Once we passed a single telephone line, dangling on rickety poles, connecting Addis Ababa to some government post; I remember resenting the slender evidence of outside interference."

attended, is still the most prestigious of British schools. And Thesiger has been able to perpetuate in his life an old-fashioned secure male-dominated world of public school and Oxbridge, Pall Mall Club and comfortable central-London flat. His world is remote from other Englands with their state schools, housing estates, holiday camps, daily commuting and dole queues. When he has travelled in distant parts, merging his identity with that of his travelling companions, he has always had this secure world in the background. Even when he spent months on end in the Iraqi marshes, he would periodically surface for a bath and a bit of English conversation at the residence of the British vice-consul in Basra.

On the other hand, he is a vagabond, dressed casually for the road and ready to live the inelegant life of wayfarers, travelling rough and travelling light. When he is far from England, he ferociously castigates Western innovations, the spearhead of global chaos, of which he sees himself an unwilling harbinger. Reminders of the West, from which he sought to escape, even in childhood upset him: "Once we passed a single telephone line, dangling on rickety poles, connecting Addis Ababa to some government post; I remember resenting the slender evidence of outside interference."

Western innovations seemed to bring in Western innovators whose crudeness of behaviour contrasted with the decorum of the uncorrupted African or Arab. In 1933 he met the Sultan of Tajura with the French commandant. "The Sultan, a good-looking young man in an immaculate white robe and closely wound white turban, had a quiet-spoken dignity, unlike our host, who waved his hands about, lit one cigarette from another, and hardly stopped talking — mostly about the advantages of a refrigerator."

"You can't really call the English or the French a noble race," he said in 1990. Nobility he found in the people he met on his travels, especially in the remoter places, and above all the Bedu of southern Arabia and the people of Oman and the Emirates. "The Bedu face the hardship of their life and nature and compete to do better than each other, more generously."

The archetypal gentleman, he nevertheless recognised and accepted the darker side of human nature. The capacity for savagery exists in everyone, himself included. Thesiger derived a "savage satisfaction" from boxing and was never conscious of pain, even when his nose was broken. It was with "savage satisfaction" in 1945 that he learned that Mussolini "had been executed by his own people and his carcass had been hung, appropriately, on a meat hook."

Savagery and the law of the jungle were controlled by ritual and kept in check by custom and respect for

T/54/29

tradition and hierarchy. To Thesiger, the headlong rush for innovation and disregard for the ways of the past are a reversal of this essential condition, and have placed the world on the brink of anarchy and self-destruction.

His comments on problems of pollution typically combine a passionate concern for humanity with a mischievously expressed drastic solution. "I think we are living right at the very edge of mankind, what with pollution and the inability to control arms proliferation. Thirty years ago," he said in June 1990, "I was saying that we cannot go on pouring poison into the seas, and the atmosphere. If you shut yourself in a room for a night with a car engine running, you would soon be dead. We've now got a billion cars doing the same thing to the earth's atmosphere. The only hope of survival for humankind is if we have some germ that wipes out five million a day and just leaves a few pockets somewhere like the rain forests. It's just like pruning a rose bush back," he added with a chuckle.

Privilege and egalitarianism; gentleness and an acknowledgement of the darker side of humanity; a personal toughness that seems almost masochistic and manners that are courtly; a pride in his country and a hostility to its role as a vehicle of Western technology to the rest of the world — Wilfred Thesiger is full of apparent contradictions. Yet a personal integrity and sincerity blaze from his eyes. He is not a philosopher and can be the first to mock himself. The bundle of paradoxes he embodies has given him the capacity to appreciate the world as it is; his gift with pen and camera has helped bring these clear-eyed perceptions into the experience of lesser mortals.

Wilfred Thesiger and companions.
When he has travelled in distant parts, merging his identity with that of his travelling companions, he has always had a secure established world in the background.

The camp.
*He found nobility in the
people he met on his travels,
above all in the Bedu of
southern Arabia.*

First visits to the Emirates

Wilfred Thesiger had always wanted to cross the Empty Quarter. The first crossings by Europeans, of this great sea of sand, had been made by Bertram Thomas and H St John Philby in the early 1930s. Thomas had crossed from Salalah to Doha; his account of the journey, *Arabia Felix*, was avidly read by Thesiger at Oxford. Philby's base had been Riyadh, where he lived as a friend of King Abdul Aziz Ibn Saud. Musallim bin Al Kamam, one of Thesiger's first and oldest companions, knew all three explorers. Years later he recalled that Thomas, whom he had known as a boy in Salalah, did not speak Arabic as well as Thesiger did, and that Philby was often in a raging temper. Thesiger, by contrast, was always calm.

Whereas Thomas had made the journey in the name of exploration, and Philby in the name of adventure, Thesiger's official reason for penetrating the all-but-impenetrable interior of Arabia was scientific. As the field worker of the Desert Locust Research Organisation, he was charged with providing an answer to a simple question: Was Arabia a breeding ground for locusts? The research would have far-reaching implications for the bread-bowl of east Africa, where crops were regularly devastated by clouds of locusts appearing from nowhere.

Locusts breed rapidly in the right conditions, the most essential of which is water. From his journeys in southern Arabia Thesiger was able to establish that rain fell in every corner of the Empty Quarter, although

sometimes at intervals of 10 or 20 years. When it did, seeds that had lain dormant for years germinated within hours and a corner of the desert would briefly support lush vegetation – and thus provide breeding conditions for the locusts.

In pursuit of the answer that yes, locusts did breed in the Empty Quarter, Thesiger was able to indulge his desire for travel and adventure. In 1945 and 1946, he made several preparatory journeys, familiarising himself with the tribes of the mountains and plains of Dhofar, the Omani region bordering the Empty Quarter to the south. Most importantly, he met the companions who were to accompany him on his greatest journeys. Among them were Musallim bin Al Kamam, Salim bin Kabina and Salim bin Ghabaisha, all men of the Rashid tribe. Thesiger felt more at home with the Rashidi than

Left. Salim bin Kabina.
The only man to have accompanied Thesiger on both crossings of the Empty Quarter.

Salim bin Ghabaisha.
An independent spirit, familiar with camels, hunting and the lore of the desert.

83/16/9

33

39/4/29

with any other tribe. "They were small, deft men," he wrote, "alert and watchful. Their bodies were lean and hard, trained to incredible endurance. Looking at them, I realised that they were very much alive, tense with nervous energy, vigorously controlled." More than any others, these Rashidi personified Arabia to Thesiger; his admiration of their simple dignity, stoic acceptance of conditions beyond their control and unfailing courtesy are common themes in his writing.

To the list of traits displayed by the Rashidi he might have added loyalty. Some 40 years later, in February 1990, these three were to make the journey to Abu Dhabi to meet Thesiger on his return to the Emirates. On that occasion, bin Kabina recalled his first impressions of Thesiger, already known then as Umbarak or Mubarak. "Umbarak was very tall," he said, "but his clothes, manner and speech were similar to the Bedu. Even his white skin was darkened by the desert sunshine and it was not easy to tell him apart from us."

Thesiger's companions first suggested that bin Kabina should join them after he had helped them dig out some water wells. "The next day I asked Umbarak to take me with him and he agreed provided I bring my

own gun and camel. That was the start of an everlasting friendship."

The first crossing of the Empty Quarter was made in late 1946. Thesiger's main guide was a Rashidi named Mohammed Al Auf and there were only three other companions, including bin Kabina, the only man who accompanied him on both epic crossings. The route took them to a point near the long crescent of oases called the Liwa, which stretched 40 miles (64 kilometres) or more, about 150 miles (240 kilometres) south-west of modern Abu Dhabi city. Thesiger was the first European to see the Liwa, the homeland of some of the major tribes of Abu Dhabi, including the ruling family, the Nahyans. From

83/14/37

the Liwa area they travelled due east, about 100 miles (160 kilometres) to the south of the Al Ain oasis back into Oman.

The second crossing was a more extensive, more adventurous and more hazardous journey which ended up at Abu Dhabi. Bin Kabina, bin Ghabaisha, two other Rashidi and two men from the Saar tribe of Manwakh, west of the Hadhramaut, accompanied him. "The adventures we had were so numerous I can't remember them all," bin Ghabaisha commented 40 years on. "We suffered a lot from hunger and thirst. We also had to hide from enemy tribes and bandits." They travelled north from Manwakh and were briefly held by Saudi officials at Sulaiyil until Philby, still living in Riyadh, personally arranged their release. They then travelled due east, south of Sabkha Mutti near the border between the Emirate of Abu Dhabi and Qatar, to a small Manasir encampment on the western edge of the Liwa. There they found a guide who would take them to Abu Dhabi.

The details of the crossings are recounted in *Arabian Sands*, an engrossing read remarkable for both content and style. Whether he is describing a desert sunset or a sandstorm, a meal of meat or the prospect of imminent starvation, Thesiger's undemonstrative language and writing never get in the way of what is, in the end, a wonderful story.

Liwa oasis.
Thesiger was the first European to see the Liwa, the homeland of some of the major tribes of Abu Dhabi.

**Crossing the Muqta to
Abu Dhabi — 1948.**

*Thesiger and his companions
reached the town of Abu
Dhabi a week after leaving
the Liwa.*

Nor was it a book written fresh after the event: He had written one or two reports after the crossings of the Empty Quarter but had not intended to write a book. When a literary agent and a publisher saw the photographs and suggested the book, he initially refused. The publisher pressed, and after a few days, Thesiger agreed. "I took all my photographs, my notebooks and some letters I had sent to my mother and went off to Denmark. I took a bedsitter in a hotel and spent several months writing it all up." Why Denmark? "I chose a place where I would have no distraction."

Although he travelled light and carried only essentials, his luggage always included a Leica II camera which he had bought in 1934. He kept it with his Ilford film in a goatskin bag to protect it from the sand. Cameras were still something of a novelty in Arabia, and Musallim bin Al Kamam recalled in recent years how Thesiger's camera was a constant topic of interest and debate.

Thesiger and his companions reached the town of Abu Dhabi on 14th March, 1948, a week after leaving the Liwa. They waded across the narrow strait onto the island of Abu Dhabi, rested by the watchtower that guarded the strait, and walked the 10 treeless miles to the sheikh's fort near the Gulf coast — the same fort which, restored and renovated, forms part of the Abu Dhabi Cultural Foundation, the site more than 40 years later of the first exhibition of Thesiger's photographs. Then, however, it was the home of the Ruler, who was asleep in the late afternoon. Thesiger and his party sat down and waited outside the walls.

In the evening they were taken into the fort, up some stairs and into the presence of Sheikh Shakhbut and his brothers, Sheikh Khalid and Sheikh Haza. They exchanged news, and Sheikh Shakhbut arranged for the party to stay in a crumbling, sparsely furnished house near the souq. Thesiger stayed in Abu Dhabi for

1950/8/16

Wilfred Thesiger with Sheikhs of Abu Dhabi — 1948.

83/12/24

three weeks, wandering along the beach and taking photographs.

The township of Abu Dhabi in those days clung to the coastline facing the Gulf. The major buildings were the sheikh's fort and a mosque built by one of the richest pearl merchants. A customs house faced the sea alongside a few other crumbling houses of stone and plaster. The other constructions were palm-frond huts (known as barasti) and boatyards.

Abu Dhabi had seen better days. The people relied for their livelihood on subsistence from the flocks of goats and camels, and dates from the oases of Al Ain and the Liwa. The sea gave them fish and the pearls which had brought relative prosperity until the world recession of the 1930s and Japanese cultured pearls sent the market crashing. The Second World War, restricting foreign trade and the import of essential foodstuffs, hit the town of Abu Dhabi hard. By the late 1940s, the population had dwindled to around 2,000.

One hundred miles inland, due east of Abu Dhabi town, lay the area known as Buraimi, which was also the name of one of the three oasis villages there giving allegiance to Oman. The other six groups of mudbrick forts and houses amid date-palm gardens, were known collectively as Al Ain, and gave their

allegiance to the Nahyan family of Abu Dhabi. The oases were a desert crossroads and trading centre, with Dubai to the north, the Omani coastal town of Sohar to the east, Ibri and the Omani mountain towns to the south-east, and the island of Abu Dhabi to the west. It was also to prove an ideal staging point for Thesiger's later expeditions into unknown territory.

In early April 1948, Thesiger set off for Al Ain with four Rashidi. They took four days from Abu Dhabi, staying the last night among the huge dunes called Hazrat Al Bush, reaching Muwaijih fort in the morning. There they were received by Sheikh Zayed bin Sultan Al Nahyan, the Ruler's brother and representative. Sheikh Zayed had held this position since 1946, rapidly building a reputation throughout the area for wisdom, shrewdness and familiarity with all aspects of desert life. His love of Bedu pastimes, camel racing and falconry cemented his relations with the tribes, and during this time he also laid the foundations for the modern city of Al Ain.

"Sheikh Zayed was sitting on the bare sand under a tree," recalled Thesiger in 1990. "He invited me to sit down but only after ordering a rug to be brought for me." Thesiger accepted Sheikh Zayed's invitation to be his guest, and stayed for nearly a

*H.H. Sheikh Shakhbut bin
Sultan bin Zayed — 1948.*

month. They shared many interests, and the result was a firm friendship that has survived to this day. For one week he camped on Jebel Hafit with bin Kabina, bin Ghabaisha and two of Sheikh Zayed's retainers, hunting tahr, an indigenous animal resembling a goat with thick short horns. Otherwise he would pass the time with Sheikh Zayed, joining him as he sat either on a bench in the porch or under a tree. They would drink coffee, receive visitors, hear the news, figure out tribal politics. Sheikh Zayed would settle disputes and give presents. Captain Bird, the representative of Petroleum Development (Trucial Coast), was staying in another village of the oasis and would sometimes come and call. "He was," wrote Thesiger, "friendly but suspicious, wondering if I was working for some rival company. I kept away from him when visiting tribesmen were about. Anyway, I was averse to all oil companies, dreading the changes and disintegration of society which they inevitably caused."

Thesiger made preparations to leave for Dubai. He planned to go to England during the summer but also wanted to penetrate Oman later in the year. He discussed his plans with Sheikh Zayed who offered encouragement and help for when he returned in the autumn. Sheikh Zayed offered to send him to Dubai in his car, but Thesiger preferred to go by camel. Sheikh Zayed then gave him the use of his camel, Ghazala, one of the finest camels in all Arabia. "Any Bedu," said one of Thesiger's companions, "would give much to say that he had ridden Ghazala."

They travelled to the coast along the edge of the sands, skirting the mountains and taking their time, shooting wild ass along the way, and reached Sharjah on 10th May. Thesiger was disgusted at the rubbish around the aerodrome and the stink of petrol fumes caused by one jeep. Sharjah then had a Royal Air Force base, and the aerodrome was a staging post en route to India. It was used by passengers of the British Overseas Airways Corporation flying-boats that touched down between marker buoys on Dubai Creek. While the flying-boat was being refuelled, passengers would be ferried to shore, and scramble onto a bus that would tear across the salt flats to Sharjah for lunch at the RAF rest house.

Left. H.H. Sheikh Zayed bin Sultan Al Nahyan — 1949.

Taking a rest.
Sheikh Zayed offered Thesiger the use of his car, but he preferred to go by camel.

Boy and falcon at Jebel Hafit.
For one week of his month-long stay in Abu Dhabi, Thesiger camped on Jebel Hafit.

39/6/13

43

Saying goodbye to his Rashidi companions for four months — they were bewildered when he changed into Western clothes — Thesiger went on to Dubai to stay with Edward Henderson.

Dubai was then the largest town of the Emirates, with a population of about 25,000. There was already a sizeable community of foreigners from further east — Indians, Baluchis and Iranians. The merchants of Dubai had good trading links with Bombay, Basra and the Iranian coast. The dhows of the Emirates went to India and Zanzibar as well as up and down the Gulf. Steamships would anchor a mile or so off Dubai to offload goods and passengers onto barges and canoes and then take on more the same way. The souqs on both sides of the creek were busy with imported goods, often sold for re-export to India or East Africa. A core of houses in Shindagha and Bur Dubai were made of coralstone and gypsum, and the skyline was broken by dozens of badgirs or windtowers. Paths and alleyways were narrow and often crowded with donkeys, camels and people of many nations. Beyond the stone buildings were acres of small

Dhows on the Dubai Creek.
Thesiger liked Dubai. There was animation. People valued leisure, courtesy and conversation.

barasti houses. In 1948 there were 24 cars in Dubai, but they were not a lot of use in the souq area — and there were of course no roads.

Thesiger liked Dubai. There was animation. People valued leisure, courtesy and conversation: "They did not live their lives at second hand." But he felt like a tourist as he wandered through the town in European clothes.

One of the many Thesiger stories, all with variations, has its origins about this time. Urbane Arab bank clerks in the Dubai branch of the British Bank of the Middle East

83/13/13

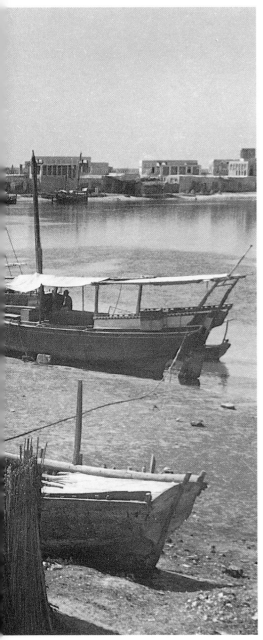

(which did not take that name until 1952) were surprised when a Bedu addressed them, in his dialect, asking to see the British manager. In the baffled silence that followed, the Bedu repeated his request, referring to the British manager by name. At this point the manager himself appeared, looked at the Bedu and said: "Is that you, Wilfred?"

Whatever the truth of the story, it was a Western-dressed Thesiger who boarded a dhow in Dubai for the voyage to Bahrain, a flight to England and an escape from the hottest months of the year and also the Muslim fasting month of Ramadan.

He returned to the Emirates in October 1948 and, reunited with Musallim bin Al Kamam, bin Kabina and bin Ghabaisha, went on a month-long journey to the Liwa. Just before Christmas 1948, Thesiger accompanied Sheikh Zayed on an expedition into the desert to hunt bustard and hare with falcons and saluki dogs. Sheikh Zayed was in his element; well-informed and generous in sharing his expertise with Thesiger.

Then, at the end of January 1949, Thesiger and his party set out from Al Ain for Oman. They cut across part of the sands which Thesiger now saw, as did his Rashidi companions, as a place of refuge. For two months they explored the mountain areas of Oman, the quicksands of Umm Al Samim and the Wahiba Sands.

Windtower houses, Dubai.
The skyline of Shindagha and Bur Dubai was broken by dozens of badgirs or windtowers.

On the Corniche, Sharjah.
*Thesiger and his companions
reached Sharjah on 10th May,
1948.*

"When I left in 1950, I felt what it was like to go into exile."

After another summer in England, Thesiger returned in November 1949 with the hope of seeing more of Oman. Once again Muwaijih was his starting point, and once again bin Kabina and bin Ghabaisha were waiting for him at Al Ain. Thesiger set off with his companions into the mountains of the Duru in Oman, then he returned to Al Ain for a few valedictory days with Sheikh Zayed. "He was always making notes and taking photographs," recalls an older resident of Al Ain. "He spent months with us and then went to Sharjah and flew away in an aeroplane and we didn't see him again."

Thesiger finally left Sheikh Zayed and travelled to Dubai full of apprehension for the future. There were, in the late 1940s, glimmers of what lay ahead. For a decade it had been believed and hoped that reserves of oil lay beneath the land or sea. Kuwait and Bahrain were already launched on the road to riches. In 1938, Sheikh Saeed of Dubai and the Rulers of Sharjah and Ras Al Khaimah had all signed agreements giving Petroleum Development (Trucial Coast) the concession to prospect for oil in their countries. The following year, Sheikh Shakhbut of Abu Dhabi had signed a similar agreement for prospecting in his much larger emirate, but the search for oil had been suspended for the duration of the war.

The principal agents of PD(TC) were men who were familiar with the local social and political scene. Not only did they have to keep on good terms with the ruling families, it was also necessary to be familiar with tribal politics and to secure at least the acquiescence, at most the cooperation, of the tribes whose territories were being invaded by cars and lorries full of surveyors, drilling crews and equipment.

In 1949, the first exploratory well in Abu Dhabi was drilled at Ras Al Sadr, 40 miles (64 kilometres) north of the island. The rest, as they say, is history and by 1965 the Gulf had replaced the United States as the world's largest producer of oil.

Thesiger had a foreboding of the changes that were to transform Arabia. He travelled to Dubai with bin Kabina and bin Ghabaisha; "I knew I would not come back and I wanted to have them with me until I left Arabia." They spent one night en route at an oil camp that had sprung up, sharing a tent in the "native lines" as his friends were barred from joining Thesiger in the "European lines".

Poignant emotion and contrast

83/10/11

marked Thesiger's final days in Arabia. He was with Edward Henderson and Ronald Codrai, two compatriots who were good-humoured and appreciative. But he was conscious of the qualities of his travelling companions from whom he was parting. "I shall always remember how often I was humbled by those illiterate herdsmen who possessed, in so much greater measure than I, generosity and courage, endurance, patience and light-hearted gallantry. Among no other people have I ever felt the same sense of personal inferiority."

When at last his two Rashidi friends departed by lorry, Thesiger embraced them for what he thought was the last time. Then he made his way to the aerodrome at Sharjah. The smell of progress tainted the desert air. "When I left in 1950," he said later, "I felt what it was like to go into exile."

Sharjah souq.
It was from Sharjah that Thesiger left Arabia in 1950.

Thesiger returns

*N*obody, not even Thesiger himself, can remember when or how he acquired the nickname Mubarak bin London. Early on in his travels in Muslim Arabia, his companions started calling this Christian in their midst Mubarak or Umbarak "bin Miriam" (son of Mary), but it is as Mubarak bin London — literally "the Blessed One from London" — that he is so widely known throughout Arabia. The people of the Emirates in particular have retained an affection for Thesiger. Mubarak bin London has been like a favourite uncle who recorded his appreciation for them before they were noticed by the rest of the world; his return in 1990 was cause for celebration.

Not without justification, his reputation has grown over the years, attaining almost mythical proportions. Thesiger himself, however, has remained a modest, dignified individual of unfailing courtesy and good manners. When confronted with his own popularity at the opening of the photo exhibition in Abu Dhabi on 10th February,1990, he commented with a smile, "I feel a bit like a pop star… like Boy George." On another occasion during that visit he was moved to say, "All this attention, the warmth of this welcome, is too much. It makes me feel almost bogus."

History will decide Thesiger's importance, and just as well, too; if it were left to him, he doubtless would write himself a minor walk-on part. It is his way to downplay his own accomplishments. Through his books, Thesiger — perhaps more than

anyone else — has helped Arabia to appreciate its own unique social history, putting into context the scale of achievement throughout the region in bridging centuries of development in the space of one generation. It is ironic that Thesiger took so long to see this for himself.

It was not difficult to recognise in the man who stepped off the flight from Kenya that February night in 1990, the same distinctive features captured in the pictures of 40 years ago, as well as the same rock-hard spirit, tempered by a gentle, self-deprecating sense of humour. Throughout the 12 hectic days of his visit — the time spent with old friends; the official engagements in Abu Dhabi, Dubai, Sharjah and Al Ain; the four-wheel-drive trip through the Hajar Mountains; the air-hop back to the Liwa; all climaxing with the opening of the Mubarak bin London photo exhibition — he proved excellent company, tireless despite his

Left and below. The two sides of Wilfred Thesiger — the formal English gentleman with the capacity to merge into other cultures — were still apparent in 1990.

ADCO

53

Enjoying dates in the Liwa with Salim bin Kabina and H.E. Mr Suhail Mazroui, General Manager of ADNOC.

80 years, willing to accommodate and gracious to a fault. At a book-signing session originally expected to last about an hour, the response was overwhelming. Over 250 of his books were sold, but Thesiger autographed many more. For more than two hours he steadily wrote his name in full as men, women and children of a dozen nationalities presented their treasured copies of his books. With people queuing to see him, he wouldn't hear of a brief respite. Echoing the resolve that carried him across the harshest part of Arabia, he said: "I'll go on until I drop if I have to."

Thesiger's mere presence cast an aura, and in a number of touching encounters, it was obvious that it had always done so. One Dubai man recalled how, on a hunting expedition in 1948, he met Thesiger and his companions at Tawi Hasan on the edge of the sands. They were mounted on camels, he was in a jeep, and to this day he remembers their scornful attitude. Another middle-aged man was able to produce a few Omani coins that he had treasured since Thesiger had given them to him as a gift in 1948. A Bedu whom Thesiger had met on his journeys welcomed him back to his tents, south of the Liwa, where he still lives the traditional life.

Of the many more who met him, however fleetingly, at the schools, clubs, embassies and private homes he visited, the words of Dr Terry Adams summed up the experience. Dr Adams, General Manager of the Abu Dhabi Company for Onshore Oil Operations (ADCO), commented about Thesiger after accompanying him back to the Liwa — in modern style and comfort — "I have met many important men, but I have met only one great man."

Among those awed by Thesiger's presence was the eminent archaeologist Dr Geoffrey King of the School of Oriental and African Studies, who had the pleasure of delivering a lecture on the ancient city of Julfar with Thesiger in the audience. It came about at a historic

Left. Amara bin Thuqub, a canoeboy in the Marshes — 1953.

Autographing books at the British Council, Dubai.

Thesiger talking to students at Rashid School in 1990. From left to right the students are Hasher Mesfer Al Amimi, Mohammed Saeed bin Atiq, Ahmed Mattar Al Arti and Tariq Obeid.

meeting of the Emirates Natural History Group.

Although Thesiger's return was celebrated in all the media, by agreement it was to remain as private a visit as possible. So when word spread that he would attend a meeting of the Emirates Natural History Group, a record crowd gathered. Group patron and Chancellor of the United Arab Emirates University, Sheikh Nahyan bin Mubarak Al Nahyan, chairing the meeting, used the occasion to describe the warmth of feeling between Thesiger and the people of the Emirates, and of the classic nature of his book, *Arabian Sands*. "Reading the book," said Sheikh Nahyan, "is an obligation for all conscientious students and travellers to the Arabian peninsula."

Then he quoted from the first introduction to *Arabian Sands*: "Others will go there to study geology and archaeology, the birds and plants and animals, even to study the Arabs themselves, but they will move about in cars and will keep in touch with the outside world by wireless. They will bring back results far more interesting than mine, but will never know the spirit of the land nor the greatness of the Arabs."

He wrote those lines close to 40 years ago, but it was a theme Thesiger would stress over and over

throughout his visit. "I have never met a community," Thesiger told journalists at a press conference, "to whom I would instinctively apply the word 'noble', other than the Bedu. I found a generosity, a hospitality, a feeling of nobility, courage, endurance, patience and good temper. What they valued above all in the desert was their freedom. It is a freedom of the spirit, with no rules and regulations except the tribal ones." He lamented, "As a result of cars and oil, Bedu life has been destroyed for ever."

But as much as that saddened him, Thesiger acknowledged that the world did not stand still, and took the opportunity to lay to rest the ghost of

Left. Fishing boat on the Marshes — 1953.

H.H. Sheikh Nahyan bin Mubarak Al Nahyan at the opening of the Emirates Natural History Group meeting in Abu Dhabi.

1953/6/23

1956/15/34

his unhappy 1977 visit. During that visit he had been "looking for the past, a past that I loved," he recalled in 1990. "The five years I spent in this part of the world were the happiest years of my life. In 1977 I did not find that past and I resented the apparent destruction of all that I had valued. I come today accepting the changes."

He said as much to Sheikh Zayed, the first evening he was in the UAE. Sheikh Zayed smiled broadly, greeted Thesiger cordially and invited him to sit beside him. Thesiger's fluent Arabic of 40 years ago failed him and he kept breaking into Swahili, the language he uses in Kenya, but the two old friends savoured the moment.

"You have done marvellous work in Abu Dhabi," said Thesiger.

"The head of a household has a duty to make his house attractive and beautiful for all his people," said Sheikh Zayed. "A fine place reflects a good spirit. You must come and live here with us," he added.

"That is very kind of you," Thesiger replied. "My book *Arabian Sands* is being translated into Arabic. I would like to thank you for all the help you have given in this. I want it to be read by young Arabs."

Soon after his arrival, Thesiger's old friends started gathering. Some, like Edward Henderson and David Heard — very much part of the planning committee — met him at the airport; others simply materialised. So it was with Musallim bin Al Kamam. Thesiger knew bin Kabina and bin Ghabaisha were expected, but surprised his hosts with the comment, "Musallim is the man I would most like to see. I have not seen him for over 40 years." Nobody knew of Musallim's whereabouts, but then out of the blue came a phone call from the British Embassy: "We have a Musallim bin Al Kamam here who wishes to see Mubarak bin London."

Musallim, a short, neatly built man with keen inquiring eyes, a trim white beard and clutching a camel stick, greeted an incredulous Thesiger with

Musallim bin Al Kamam.

ADCO

a nose kiss. They had first met in January 1946. Musallim was then in his 20s, already a sheikh of the Rashidi who had travelled extensively and gained a reputation throughout southern Arabia as a peace-maker among tribes. Indeed, his stature was greater than Thesiger's in certain circles. A story tells how in 1947 in inner Oman, Thesiger was pointed out as a Christian and an old man asked: "Is he the Christian who travelled last year with bin Al Kamam and the Rashidi to the Hadhramaut?" Today Musallim lives at Thumrait in Dhofar, where word had reached him of Thesiger's return. He had travelled to Abu Dhabi by shared taxi.

Musallim joined Thesiger at the Abu Dhabi Cultural Foundation, where the photo exhibition was to be held, to preview the enlargements of his photos. They paused at a picture of a Bedu alone on a sand dune peering into the distance. Musallim looked at Thesiger.

Left above. A mudhif (guest house) at Hamar at the time of heavy floods — 1953.

Left below. Inside a mudhif on the Euphrates — 1956.

Thesiger looked at Musallim. "That's me," murmured Musallim.

The next to arrive was Salim bin Kabina, making a flamboyant entrance at a press conference. Thesiger had been describing his experiences of 40 years ago to journalists seated around a table. "We were constantly worried by what would happen if our camels died. There was the threat of raiders and the Duru drove us out of their country on two occasions," he said. "In such circumstances you inevitably develop a close relationship with your travelling companions. My companions, bin Kabina, bin Ghabaisha and Musallim bin Al Kamam — no people ever mattered to me more than they did."

No sooner had he spoken, than a piercing, shrill, drawn-out greeting of "As salaam-o-alaykum" broke the calm, and in strode bin Kabina in flowing Bedu robes. The controlled atmosphere of the press conference gave way to a gleeful reunion of old friends. The Rashidi were perplexed that Thesiger had lost his fluency in Arabic. "I always did say that the English age so quickly," laughed bin Kabina, the only man to have accompanied Thesiger on both crossings of the Empty Quarter. He had been about 16 when he joined

Thesiger's group in 1946, desperately poor then, with the hardships of his life etched in his hollow face. Today bin Kabina lives at Wadi Qitbit in Dhofar, on the edge of the sands.

"I still have my camels," he told Thesiger, "but I also have a jeep."

"What — no Mercedes?" laughed Thesiger. "Thank God!"

At dinner, the old relationship of a teenager's deference to Umbarak persisted as bin Kabina selected the juiciest morsels of meat from the dish and undemonstratively passed them on to Thesiger. "He was a good friend to me when times were good and

Musallim bin Al Kamam and Wilfred Thesiger have their memories stirred by their first sight of the photographs. H.E. Mr Abdul Rahim Mahmud looks on.

Left. A Duru — 1949.

Salim bin Kabina.

Terence Clark

bad," recalled bin Kabina.

"The only thing wrong with Umbarak," commented bin Kabina, "is that he has not had a family."

"I could not have had the life I have had if I had been married," replied Thesiger.

By contrast, when bin Ghabaisha arrived by plane, he was met at the airport and taken to a modern hotel. But he found the hotel a frightening and alien institution and moved out to stay with fellow tribesmen. Bin Ghabaisha had first turned up with bin Kabina before the second crossing of the Empty Quarter. The same age as his friend, he was an independent spirit, familiar with camels, hunting and the lore of the desert. In the early 1950s bin Ghabaisha gained a reputation in Sharjah as a notorious brigand, but today he lives a quieter life in Dhofar.

With his "Three Musketeers" around him, Thesiger thought he was ready for the formal opening of his photo exhibition by Sheikh Nahyan bin Mubarak Al Nahyan. But nothing could have prepared him for that memorable evening. Five hundred had been invited, but estimates put the throng at between 1,000 and 1,500: Sheikhs and Bedu, former ministers and present ambassadors, old friends of Thesiger, new friends, nationals, foreigners… Many wished no more than to set eyes on this gaunt, shy, slightly embarrassed old man. Cameras flashed, television crews swayed with the crowd.

In the presence of dignitaries including Sheikh Nahyan; British Ambassador Graham Burton; Andrew Buxton, of Barclays Bank, whose sponsorship made the event possible; and Sir Richard Francis, Director-General of the British Council; Thesiger spoke briefly and eloquently. The desert hardships, he said, brought out qualities to be cherished. All that is best in the Arab character came from the desert. The applause was prolonged and affectionate.

Thesiger's remarkable pictures struck a common chord with all who

Terence Clark

Left. Salim bin Ghabaisha.

Far left. In a dhow at Abu Dhabi — 1948.

Below. Thesiger and H.H. Sheikh Nahyan bin Mubarak Al Nahyan opening and touring the photo exhibition in Abu Dhabi.

83/8/37

64

saw them; a superb historical record of places whose names are familiar but whose appearance has been transformed, they also show people as they were at the end of an era that had lasted for centuries. The natives of the Emirates were fascinated by the minutiae of the photos. Sometimes it was in identifying people or observing half-forgotten details, but in total the contrast between the life frozen in black and white and that of today could hardly be greater. They looked, understood, and accepted. An old sheikh later remarked that Thesiger and his pictures had been the talk of the majlises for weeks.

After Abu Dhabi, the exhibition moved to Dubai, Sharjah, Al Ain and Ras Al Khaimah, opening each time with renewed ceremony and interest. In Sharjah, the Ruler, H.H. Dr Sheikh Sultan bin Mohammed Al Qasimi, cut the ribbon, as did the Ras Al Khaimah Ruler, H.H. Sheikh Saqr bin Mohammed Al Qasimi, in his Emirate. But long before any of this, Thesiger had returned to Kenya. He spent the last few days of his visit in Abu Dhabi in the company of the men whose companionship meant so much to him, then departed as he had come, quietly and informally.

"I have been overwhelmed and amazed," Thesiger said in a press statement issued as he left, "by the warmth of the welcome I have received on this visit to the Emirates. It has been a moving experience to meet so many old friends."

"I have been most impressed by the dignity of Abu Dhabi city," he continued. "I wish to pay tribute to the amazing achievement of my old

H.H. Dr Sheikh Sultan bin Mohammed Al Qasimi discusses a point with the author at the opening of the exhibition in Sharjah.

Left. Boy with a rifle during the first crossing of the Empty Quarter — 1947.

H.H. Sheikh Tahnoun bin Mohammed Al Nahyan with the author at the opening of the exhibition in Al Ain.

H.H. Sheikh Saqr bin Mohammed Al Qasimi cuts the tape at the opening of the exhibition in Ras Al Khaimah.

friend, Sheikh Zayed bin Sultan Al Nahyan, in creating the modern Abu Dhabi." Thanking everyone, especially Sheikh Zayed, for their hospitality, he expressed the hope that the Arabic translation of *Arabian Sands* would be read by a younger generation of Arabs "who wish to know how their fathers and grandfathers lived."

If Thesiger has happy memories of the Emirates, so too do they have a place in their heart for him. "Friendship lasts for ever," Sheikh Zayed had said to him the first night of his visit. "Whatever happens to people, happy memories remain for ever. You are unforgettable."

Left. Boy with a goatskin of water for sale in the souq — Kuwait, 1949.

39/21/33

Epilogue

by Ian Fairservice

Twenty months later, Thesiger paid another visit to southern Arabia. The occasion was the launch of the long-awaited official Arabic version of *Arabian Sands*, a project which had received generous financial support from Thesiger's old friend, H.H. Sheikh Zayed bin Sultan Al Nahyan, President of the United Arab Emirates. This publication coincided with the issue of *The Thesiger Collection*, a catalogue of his photographs that were now available for the first time to the public.

He spent four days in Oman where the British Council in Muscat had arranged an exhibition of his Oman photographs. And in Dubai, the popular collection of his photographs of the Emirates was once again exhibited at the British Council there.

As Thesiger's Middle East publishers, it was our privilege to invite him back to Arabia, and to arrange the busy two-week schedule that followed his arrival in the early hours of 15th October, 1991. Now 81 years old, frailer than he had been the previous year, with failing eyesight, Thesiger was nevertheless as alert as ever and, if anything, more relaxed.

During his visit, I had the honour of accompanying Thesiger to the desert palace of Sheikh Zayed at Rawdat Al Reed, and on this occasion our party included Peter Clark and Thesiger's old friend Edward Henderson. Here Thesiger presented Sheikh Zayed with an autographed copy of *Arabian Sands* in Arabic, inscribed 'In remembrance of past times'.

Sheikh Zayed leafed through *The Thesiger Collection*, chuckling and identifying people and places. "We were all amazed at what you did," he mused. "You came from the settled lands and lived among us, accepting all the hardships and deprivations of the Bedu. People could not believe it. Your name will live for ever."

Left. A smiling Wahiba face — Oman 1949.

H.H. Sheikh Zayed bin Sultan Al Nahyan with, from right to left, Ian Fairservice, Wilfred Thesiger and Edward Henderson.

71

Thesiger agreed that they were difficult times. "People were always on the alert. The Bedu were close to each other. If others approached we would fire two shots into the air."

"And we would wave like this," said Sheikh Zayed, sweeping his right hand slowly and broadly over his head.

"And when they were closer we would pick up a handful of sand and throw it into the air, as a gesture of friendship," added Thesiger, tossing an imaginary handful of sand.

Sheikh Zayed asked if he still hunted, but Thesiger explained that his eyes had become too weak now.

"You used to be an excellent shot — better than I was at 400 metres," Sheikh Zayed responded.

One of the most popular pictures of the 1990 exhibition had been the smiling face of Sheikh Tahnoun bin Mohammed Al Nahyan, then a 10-year-old boy and now the Ruler's Representative in the Eastern Region. Welcoming Thesiger to Al Ain, Sheikh Tahnoun recalled those earlier days vividly. "You used to have a dog," he reminded Thesiger, even remembering its name — Warrad — where Thesiger could not. The name means one who wanders around extensively; perhaps the Arabic equivalent of Rover. "I remember how short we were of food in those days," Sheikh Tahnoun went on. "One day Warrad stole some meat. We had to chase him and take it from his mouth!"

In Al Ain, Thesiger spoke to schoolchildren at the English Speaking Primary School who had grouped themselves into three houses named after famous explorers: American astronaut Neil Armstrong, French underwater legend Jacques Cousteau — and Wilfred Thesiger. The children had written to him, and in his reply he had promised to visit them when he next came to the Emirates. Fulfilling his pledge, Thesiger faced searching questions from his young admirers: Do you like camels? Did you use maps or did you rely on tracks and your travelling companions? Were you hungry? If it was difficult for the children to fathom the almost unbelievable hardships of just 40 years

Ian Fairservice

ago, equally it was hard to take in the enormity of the progress that made it possible for them and their school to exist in the area that Thesiger was describing.

It was the same in Oman. Modern Muscat, incorporating spectacular roads and buildings into its naturally magnificent surroundings, is a far cry from the Oman Thesiger explored 40 years ago. But the Omani authorities are active in preserving vital elements of a rich national heritage, like the great forts of both coast and interior, to ensure that they will be there for future generations to appreciate. One such monument is Jalali Fort, which guards one side of the entrance to Muscat harbour, and overlooks the hundred-year-old British Embassy residence where Thesiger and I stayed as the guests of Ambassador Sir Terence Clark and Lady Clark.

Whereas in Abu Dhabi, the previous year, Thesiger had seemed uncomfortable with his celebrity status, he showed no such signs in what was to be a whirlwind four days in Oman. Perhaps it was the effect of seeing again his old travelling companions, Salim bin Kabina, Salim bin Ghabaisha and Sheikh Musallim bin Tafl who were there to greet him at Seeb international airport, along with representatives of the Omani government. The next generation of Omanis was also there in

Wilfred Thesiger on the verandah of the British Embassy residence beside Jalali Fort in Muscat.

Left. Sheikh Tahnoun — Al Ain 1948.

the person of Said Al Rashidi, son of Thesiger's friend Musallim bin Al Kamam. Bin Al Kamam had come to Abu Dhabi in 1990, but at the time of this visit was in India for medical treatment. Thesiger was pleased to learn that his son, Said, a graduate in geology from the University of Qatar, was working for the Wali of Salalah on water resources.

Much was packed into Thesiger's short visit: He called on members of the Omani government; was honoured at lunches and dinners by Omanis and British, including an embassy lunch with the officers of the H.M.S. Scylla; he held a well-attended press conference and gave radio and television interviews; and at the one book-signing session arranged, laboured non-stop for more than an hour to make sure nobody was disappointed.

The exhibition of Thesiger's Oman photographs was mounted at the Cultural Club at Al Qurm and officially opened by H.H. Sayed Faisal, Minister of National Heritage and Culture. At the opening, Thesiger made a brief and moving speech recalling his love and appreciation of the people of Oman and southern Arabia.

But for Thesiger, always a private person who prefers the small gesture to the grand occasion, it was the hours spent again in the company of his old friends that made the trip worthwhile. This time, on their home territory, bin

Terence Clark

Kabina, bin Ghabaisha and bin Tafl hosted a traditional Arabic luncheon for Thesiger. He was in his element. After the meal, Thesiger presented each of his old companions with a bisht, the traditional Arab cloak, and from them received, appropriately, a camel saddle and goatskin water carrier. It was an emotional moment when the light of affection transcended the marks left by the passage of time on the faces and figures of Thesiger and his friends.

No visit by Thesiger to Oman — where, after all, his celebrated affair with Arabia began in 1946 — could be complete without returning to the interior. So it was that early in the

Said Al Rashidi, son of Musallim bin Al Kamam.

Left. Wahiba girl at a well — Oman 1949.

Thesiger presenting bishts to his old companions, Salim bin Ghabaisha, Musallim bin Tafl and Salim bin Kabina.

1950/8/24

morning of Thesiger's final day in Oman, our party including bin Kabina, bin Ghabaisha and bin Tafl climbed into Embassy Land Rovers for the journey to the old capital of Nizwa. The route up Wadi Sumail in the shadow of Jebel Akhdar, the highest mountain in Arabia, was not unfamiliar to Thesiger, but the feats of road engineering that made it possible to take in Nizwa and the old fort at Birkat Al Mauz in one day were a revelation. Thesiger was impressed, and at the same time grateful that development had not completely destroyed the fabric of village life that was so much a part of his Oman.

Someone like Thesiger, returning to Arabia after a long absence, cannot fail to be confronted by the much-commented-upon physical changes which have taken place over the past 40 years. It is only on closer contact with the people, however, that it becomes apparent that some things — the most important things — never change. The basic tenets of Arabian hospitality remain intact and customs such as exchanging personal gifts are still dear to those who could not hold back the tide of progress. Thesiger, recognising this, could take heart. When the last of the never-ending handshakes of farewell had finally been unclasped, his departure was that of a man who, knowing how it felt to be exiled, could now go in peace.

Ian Bailey

Above. Thesiger with bin Kabina, bin Tafl and bin Ghabaisha at Birkat Al Mauz.

Far left. Bin Kabina and bin Ghabaisha — Oman 1950.

Ian Fairservice

Left. These children will inherit a very different Oman from the country Thesiger travelled 40 years ago, but the basic tenets of Arabian culture remain unchanged.

The Empty Quarter — 1948.

99/9/36

Acknowledgements

*T*hanks and appreciation go, above all, to His Highness Sheikh Zayed bin Sultan Al Nahyan, President of the United Arab Emirates and Ruler of Abu Dhabi, who hosted the visit of Wilfred Thesiger to the United Arab Emirates in February 1990.

I am also grateful to His Highness Dr Sheikh Sultan bin Mohammed Al Qasimi, Member of the Supreme Council of the UAE and Ruler of Sharjah, for opening the exhibition in Sharjah; to His Highness Sheikh Saqr bin Mohammed Al Qasimi, Member of the Supreme Council and Ruler of Ras Al Khaimah, for opening the exhibition in Ras Al Khaimah; to His Highness Sheikh Nahyan bin Mubarak Al Nahyan for opening the exhibition in Abu Dhabi; to His Highness Sheikh Hasher bin Maktoum Al Maktoum for opening the exhibition in Dubai, and to His Highness Sheikh Tahnoun bin Mohammed Al Nahyan for opening the exhibition in Al Ain.

His Excellency Mr Ahmad Khalifa Al Suwaidi, supported by His Excellency Mr Abdul Rahm Mahmoud, Dr Ahmad Humaidan, Mr Ibrahim Bumjid and Ms Khulud Muhammad Ali, ensured that the visit was happy and successful.

His Excellency Mr Suhail Faris Mazroui, General Manager of Abu Dhabi National Oil Company, gave generously in terms of time, facilities and friendship during the weekend in the Liwa.

His Highness Sheikh Mubarak bin Mohammed Al Nahyan, His Excellency Humaid bin Drai and Mr Muhammad Al Murr provided memorable entertainment.

The series of exhibitions would not have been possible without generous financial support from Barclays Bank Plc. I am grateful to Mr Andrew Buxton, Vice-Chairman, to Mr Peter Watford and Mr Vincent Cook of the Dubai branch, and to Mr Abbas Khawaja of the Sharjah branch for their assistance.

Enabling help was provided by Mr Michael Shaw of Curtis Brown and John Farquharson, by Ms Carol O'Brien, Mr Ronald Clark and Ms Lucinda McNeile of Collins and by Mr Patrick Skinner of EPR International. Help in mounting the exhibition was provided locally by Mrs Donna Goth and Ms Julia Williams.

Mr Michael Hall and Shell gave financial support to enable Salim bin Ghabaisha to visit Abu Dhabi.

Mr Edward Henderson, C.M.G., and Mrs Jocelyn Henderson provided a link with Wilfred Thesiger's past. Both were unfailingly supportive.

Dr Terry Adams, General Manager of the Abu Dhabi Company for Onshore Oil Operations, made exhaustive and punctilious arrangements to ensure that Wilfred Thesiger's visit to the Liwa would be more comfortable but no less memorable than his first. To him and his colleagues many thanks.

Mr Peter Hellyer was an understanding friend, ever helpful when help was most required.

Mr Jolyon Kay and Mrs Shirley Kay readily offered their hospitality in Dubai at a time which cannot have been too convenient for them.

Mr Ian Fairservice of Motivate Publishing and Mr John Henen of the Rashid School helped to make Wilfred Thesiger feel at home in Dubai.

I am grateful for the collective support of British Council colleagues and friends who worked generously and enthusiastically to guarantee a successful exhibition and event. Sir Richard Francis, K.C.M.G., Director General, showed his appreciation of the historic importance of the occasion by accompanying Wilfred Thesiger to the Liwa and at the opening of the exhibition in Abu Dhabi. For their various contributions, I wish to thank Suzie and Allen Swales, Andrew McNab and Stephen Bremner of Dubai; Sue and Gary Evans of Al Ain; Roger Davis of Nairobi; and Maggie Williams, Marie-Reine Shehayed, Ramamurthi and Packir Muhammad of Abu Dhabi.

Support and encouragement were constantly provided by Mr and Mrs Graham Burton, Mr Norman Cameron and Dr Robert Wilson of the British Embassy, Abu Dhabi.

No words will adequately express all that is owed to Theresa, Frauke and David.

And finally, I would like to thank **BP Exploration** whose sponsorship has made possible the publication of this book.

Bibliography

Author

Books
ADCO: Oil, *A Dream Comes True* (ADCO, Abu Dhabi, 1988)

Erhard F Gabriel (ed): *The Dubai Handbook* (Institute for Applied Economic Geography, Ahrensburg, 1987)

Frauke Heard-Bey: *From Trucial States to United Arab Emirates* (Longman, London, 1982)

Edward Henderson: *This Strange Eventful History* (Quartet, London, 1988)

Raymond O'Shea: *The Sand Kings of Oman* (Methuen, London, 1947)

Wilfred Thesiger: *Arabian Sands* (Longman, London, 1959)
Wilfred Thesiger: *The Marsh Arabs* (Longman, London, 1964)
Wilfred Thesiger: *Desert Marsh and Mountain* (Collins, London, 1979)
Wilfred Thesiger: *The Life of My Choice* (Collins, London, 1987)
Wilfred Thesiger: *Visions of a Nomad* (Collins, London, 1987)

Articles
Abdullah Abdul Rahman: 'Mubarak bin London, Lover of the Liwa' (in Arabic), *Al Ittihad*, Abu Dhabi, 15th February, 1990.

Peter Beaumont: Interview with Wilfred Thesiger, *The Observer*, London, 3rd June, 1990.

Peter Hellyer: 'Return to the Sands', *Emirates News*, Abu Dhabi, 17th February, 1990.

Abdul Rahman Naqi: Interview with Musallim bin Al Kamam (in Arabic), *Al Bayan*, Dubai, 3rd June, 1990.

Abbas G. Rasool: 'Arabian Sands Revisited' in *PDO News*, Muscat, 1987.

Peter Clark was born in Sheffield in 1939. He has degrees in history and has studied Arabic over the last 20 years.
The author of *Marmaduke Pickthall: British Muslim* (Quartet, London, 1986), Peter Clark has also translated, from Arabic into English, selected stories by the Dubai writer Muhammad Al Murr, which were published as *Dubai Tales* (Forest Books, London, 1991).
He is married with three sons and a step-daughter, and has worked for the British Council since 1967, mostly in the Arab world.
After four years in the UAE as Director of the British Council, his next assignment is to reopen British Council operations in Syria and Lebanon.

The Thesiger Collection

If you have enjoyed the photographs in *Thesiger's Return*, you may be interested to know that Motivate Publishing also publishes *The Thesiger Collection*, a catalogue of 136 unique photographs by this great explorer, from which hand-finished photographic prints from the original negatives can be ordered.

Motivate Publishing is now extending this exclusive arrangement to include all the prints in *Thesiger's Return* which carry reference numbers.

These rare photographs provide a unique record of the legendary travels of one of the great explorers of the twentieth century. Hand-finished photographic prints from the original negatives can be ordered from this catalogue.

Catalogue price refunded with first order

Certificate of Authenticity

The Empty Quarter–1948 Ref. 99/9/11

An original, hand-finished photographic print from

The Thesiger Collection

Taken from the original negative, this rare photograph provides a unique record of the legendary travels of this great explorer in the mid-twentieth century.

Wilfred Thesiger CBE

This print has been produced for private display only, is subject to international copyright law and may not be reproduced in any form.

An individually signed certificate of authenticity, also suitable for framing, accompanies each print.

Prints from *The Thesiger Collection* and *Thesiger's Return* can be ordered in a variety of sizes:
16" x 12" = Dhs 600 or £95;
20" x 16" = Dhs 850 or £135;
40" x 30" = Dhs 1400 or £220.
Larger prints are also available and priced on request.

The individually hand-finished and retouched 16" x 12" and 20" x 16" prints are supplied masked and mounted for framing; larger sizes are unmounted and rolled in a protective tube.

To place an order, please write to Motivate Publishing, quoting the relevant reference numbers and descriptions, as well as the sizes required. Please also enclose full payment and your address and telephone number.
Cheques should be made payable to Motivate Publishing.
Delivery will take approximately four weeks.

Copyright of these photographs rests with Wilfred Thesiger. Prints are supplied for display purposes only, and may not be reproduced.

MOTIVATE
P U B L I S H I N G

P.O. Box 2331, Dubai, United Arab Emirates,
Tel: (04) 824060, Fax: (04) 824436
P.O.Box 43072, Abu Dhabi, United Arab Emirates,
Tel: (02) 311666, Fax: (02) 311888
London House, 26/40 Kensington High Street, London W8 4PF,
Tel: 071 937 4024 Fax: 071 937 7293

NB. Prices and exchange rates are subject to change.

Arabian Profiles
edited by Ian Fairservice
and Chuck Grieve

Land of the Emirates
by Shirley Kay

Enchanting Oman
by Shirley Kay

Bahrain — Island Heritage
by Shirley Kay

Dubai — Gateway to the Gulf
edited by Ian Fairservice

**Abu Dhabi — Garden City
of the Gulf**
edited by Ian Fairservice
and Peter Hellyer

Fujairah — An Arabian Jewel
by Peter Hellyer

Portrait of Ras Al Khaimah
by Shirley Kay

Sharjah — Heritage and Progress
by Shirley Kay

**Architectural Heritage
of the Gulf**
by Shirley Kay
and Dariush Zandi

**Emirates Archaeological
Heritage**
by Shirley Kay

Gulf Landscapes
by Elizabeth Collas
and Andrew Taylor

Mammals of the Southern Gulf
by Christian Gross

The Living Desert
by Marycke Jongbloed

Seashells of Southern Arabia
by Donald and Eloise Bosch

The Living Seas
by Frances Dipper
and Tony Woodward

Sketchbook Arabia
by Margaret Henderson

The Thesiger Collection
a catalogue of unique photographs
by Wilfred Thesiger

Thesiger's Return
by Peter Clark

Juha — Last of the Errant Knights
by Mustapha Kamal,
translated by Jack Briggs

Fun in the Emirates
by Aisha Bowers
and Leslie P. Engelland

Mother Without a Mask
by Patricia Holton

**Library boxes and boxed sets
are also available**

MOTIVATE
PUBLISHING

Arabian Albums

**Dubai
An Arabian Album**
by Ronald Codrai

Premier Editions

A Day Above Oman
by John Nowell

Land of the Emirates
by Shirley Kay

Enchanting Oman
by Shirley Kay

Dubai — Gateway to the Gulf
edited by Ian Fairservice

**Abu Dhabi — Garden
City of the Gulf**
edited by Ian Fairservice
and Peter Hellyer

Arabian Heritage
Guides

**Snorkelling and Diving
in Oman**
by Rod Salm and Robert Baldwin

**The Green Guide
to the Emirates**
by Marycke Jongbloed

Off-Road in the Emirates
by Dariush Zandi

Off-Road in Oman
by Heiner Klein
and Rebecca Brickson